Best Easy Day Hikes Series

best
easy
dayhikes
Aspen

Tracy Salcedo-Chourré

FALCONGUIDE®

GUILFORD, CONNECTICUT
HELENA, MONTANA

AN IMPRINT OF THE GLOBE PEQUOT PRESS

A **FALCON** GUIDE®

Library of Congress Cataloging-in-Publication data is available.

ISBN-13: 978-0-7627-2271-6
ISBN-10: 0-7627-2271-1

Manufactured in the United States of America
First Edition/Second Printing

Contents

Dedication

This book is dedicated to Sarah B. Chourré and the memory of Jules Emile "Bud" Chourré. Their love of hiking and backpacking is both inspired and inspiring.

Acknowledgments

I am indebted to the following folks, whose support and expertise were integral to the production of this book, in both its incarnations: Charlie Bean of the Aspen office, White River National Forest; Dan Matthews, Wilderness Ranger, Aspen Ranger District, White River National Forest; Grace Gary, Director, Aspen Historical Society; George Meyers and Merrill Wilson; Karen, Scott, Jake, and Cody Charland; Sara, Elliot, Gus, and Emma Bruhl; Sarah B. Chourré; Angela Logan; Chris Salcedo; Sandy Weiner; Nancy Salcedo; my parents Judy and Jesse Salcedo; my stalwart sons Jesse, Cruz, and Penn; and, most of all, my husband Martin Chourré, whose help and support were invaluable. If I forgot anyone, my apologies. Thank you all.

Map Legend

State or Other Principal Road	⑧⑧ ⑧⑧	Campground	▲
Paved Road	⟹	Picnic Area	⊓
Gravel Road	⟹	Peak	🏔 9,782 ft.
Four-wheel-drive Road	= = = = ⟹	Trailhead	◯
Main Trail	••‿••‿••	Cabin/Building	■
Secondary Trail	‿•‿•‿•	City	⊞ **City**
Boardwalk	ıııııılllllıı	View/Overlook	⋟
Parking	Ⓟ	Pass/Saddle	) (
River/Creek/Waterfall	‿⧵⧵‿	Continental Divide	⋯
Bridge	‿⌣	Wilderness Boundary	⌐⌐⌐
Meadow/Marsh	⣄		
Prospect/Mine	✕	Map Orientation	N ▲
Airport	✈		
Cemetery	†	Scale	0 0.5 1 Miles
Gate	•—•		

Overview Map

To Glenwood Springs

Old Snowmass

Roaring Fork River

Snowmass Road

Woody Creek

Capitol Creek Road

Snowmass Creek Road

82

Hardscrabble Lake ①

Williams Lake

Brush Creek Road

Snowmass Village

To Woody Creek

②

Owl Creek Road

⑤

Haystack Mountain 12,206 ft.

④ ③
Snowmass Ski Area

Sardy Air Field

Roundabout

Capitol Peak 14,130 ft.

Elk Mountains

MAROON BELLS– SNOWMASS WILDERNESS

Maroon Creek

Castle Creek

Snowmass Mountain 14,091 ft.

Maroon Lake

⑪

⑩

Crater Lake ⑫

North Maroon Peak 14,014 ft.

East Maroon Creek

Pyramid Peak 14,018 ft.

Maroon Peak 14,156 ft.

Cathedral Peak 13,943 ft.

West Maroon Creek

⑬

Cathedral Lake

Aspen Area

0   2.5   5
Miles

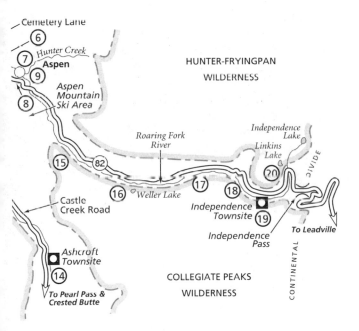

Cemetery Lane
⑥
⑦ *Hunter Creek*
Aspen
⑨
⑧
Aspen
Mountain
Ski Area

HUNTER-FRYINGPAN
WILDERNESS

*Roaring Fork
River*

*Independence
Lake*

*Linkins
Lake*

⑮   ㉒
⑳

DIVIDE

⑯ *Weller Lake*   ⑰   ⑱

Castle
Creek Road

Independence
Townsite ⑲

Independence
Pass

To Leadville

⑭

Ashcroft
Townsite

*To Pearl Pass &
Crested Butte*

COLLEGIATE PEAKS
WILDERNESS

CONTINENTAL

Ranking the Hikes

In the list that follows, hikes in this guide are ranked from easiest to hardest based on trail length, elevation change, and difficulty of the terrain.

Introduction

Fabulous sights are commonplace in Aspen—movie stars, world-class athletes, political powerhouses, private jets and stretch limousines, ostentatious homes and outrageous fashion...

... and mountains, glorious mountains. The hikes described in this guide allow you to savor the rosy beauty of the renowned Maroon Bells, climb into the sharp-toothed basins of Independence Pass, and plunge into thick, dark forests of pine and fir along Maroon Creek. Enjoy a peaceful ramble along the shores of the Roaring Fork River near downtown Aspen, take on challenging switchbacks that lead up to a rock outcrop overlooking the Roaring Fork Valley, and lose yourself in the nostalgia of the Independence Townsite or the ghost town of Ashcroft. And when the hike is over, rejuvenate with fine cuisine in one of the town's restaurants, relax in a hot bubbling spa, and collapse into a soft, quiet bed.

It's all fabulous.

The hikes in this book represent a small selection of what is available in the mountains around Aspen. They are, for the most part, very easy. Most are less than five miles in length, and a couple are short wanderings through ghost towns, but many link to backcountry routes in the surrounding wilderness, and beckon further exploration. With a good U.S. Geological Survey topographic map and a desire to explore, you can venture to destinations beyond those described here.

While I am very comfortable calling these hikes the best, calling them easy is a bit more problematic. Easy, in the mountains, is a relative term—nearly all of these hikes involve some climbing or descending, sometimes steeply, rendering their qualification as "easy" entirely subjective. To aid in the selection of a hike that suits particular needs and abilities, I have ranked them from easiest to hardest. Keep in mind that even the steepest of these trails can be made "easy" by knowing your limits and taking frequent rests.

This guide is an expansion of a book I wrote in 1995 for Chockstone Press. That guide, *12 Short Hikes Aspen*, described routes that took less than two hours to enjoy. This limitation sometimes resulted in what some may consider truncated hikes, especially on those trails, like Sunnyside, Hunter Creek, and Difficult Creek, which stretch farther into the surrounding wildernesses. Where possible, I have added options in this guide that describe how you can extend your hike to another destination.

In researching the new hikes included here, I was struck again by the awesome high-country landscapes surrounding Aspen. I hiked under flawless blue skies and in the shadows of rumbling thunderstorms, through the moist riparian habitat of Maroon Creek, and into the high, wind-scoured basin of Cathedral Lake, reveling in the variety and the grandeur of the terrain. Aspen, for all its glitz and kitsch, draws its most enduring beauty from the raw power of the Rockies, and my hope is that those who hike in these wild-lands will ponder, if only for a moment, the vast difference between the power of nature and the power of money.

—*Tracy Salcedo-Chourré*

2

How to Use This Guide

Hiking is generally a straightforward affair: pick a trail, lace up the boots, and put one foot in front of the other. This guide is intended to be just as straightforward, but these brief notes on organization and resources will hopefully make your journey even more pleasurable.

Each hike described herein is within an hour's drive of the roundabout on Colorado Highway 82, at its junction with Castle Creek Road and Maroon Creek Road. The hikes are generally arranged from northwest (down the valley) to southeast (up the valley), and from north to south up Maroon and Castle Creeks.

Several great maps to the Aspen area are available, including those produced by National Geographic/Trails Illustrated, Latitude 40, and, of course, the U.S. Geological Survey. Check out any of the wonderful out doors stores in the Aspen area, or visit the White River National Forest Aspen Ranger District office at 806 West Hallam in Aspen; (970) 925-3445. The Forest Service identifies its trails with both names and numbers; those numbers are listed where applicable. I have listed the relevant USGS topo maps in the hiking descriptions, but some of these trails are not shown on the topos. Features surrounding the trails do appear on the maps, however.

In addition to turning you on to the best maps of the area, the rangers at the Aspen Ranger District office are kindly and knowledgeable. I would advise any hiker venturing into unknown territory to first check with the rangers; they can advise you on current trail conditions, potential closures, and other details that might be pertinent. For general information, you can also visit the website at www.fs.fed.us/r2/whiteriver/virtual_vc.html.

To determine how long it might take you to complete any of these hikes, consider that on flat ground, most hikers average 2 miles per hour. Adjust that rate by the level of difficulty and your fitness level (subtract time if you are an aerobic animal and add time if you are traveling with kids), and you have a ballpark hiking duration. Add more time if you plan to go birding, picnic, or partake of some other extracurricular activity.

Zero Impact

The trails that weave through Aspen and the backcountry that surrounds the town are quite heavily used in the summer months, and sometimes take a real beating. Because of their popularity, we, as trail users and advocates, must be especially vigilant to make sure our passing leaves no lasting mark.

Equate traveling these trails to visiting a museum. You obviously would avoid leaving a mark on any art treasure in the museum. If everyone who visited the museum left one tiny mark, the art would be destroyed—and what would a building full of trashed art be worth? The same goes for these trails. If we all left just one little mark on the landscape, the parks and wildlands would soon be despoiled.

These trails can accommodate plenty of human travel if everybody treats them with respect. Just a few thoughtless, badly mannered, or uninformed visitors can ruin them for everyone who follows. The book *Leave No Trace* is a valuable resource for learning more about these principles.

Three Falcon Zero-Impact Principles
- *Leave with everything you brought.*
- *Leave no sign of your visit.*
- *Leave the landscape as you found it.*

Litter is the scourge of all trails. It is unsightly, polluting, and potentially dangerous to wildlife. Pack out all of your own trash, including biodegradable items like orange peels, which might be sought out by area critters. You might also pack out garbage left trailside by less considerate hikers.

Do not approach or feed any wild creatures—the ground squirrel eyeing your snack food is best able to survive if it remains self-reliant, because it is not likely to find an energy bar along the trail when winter comes.

Please, do not pick the wildflowers—or gather rocks, antlers, feathers, and other treasures you see along the trail. Removing these items will only take away from the next hiker's backcountry experience.

Avoid damaging trailside soils and plants by remaining on the established routes. To avoid promoting erosion, do not cut switchbacks. Leaving the trail also may mean trampling fragile vegetation, especially at high altitude. Select durable surfaces, like rocks, logs, or sandy areas, for resting spots.

Be courteous by not making loud noises while hiking.

Some of these trails are multi-use, which means you will share them with other hikers, trail runners, mountain bikers, and equestrians. Familiarize yourself with the proper trail etiquette, yielding the trail when appropriate.

If possible, use outhouses at trailheads or along the trail. If facilities are not available, pack in a lightweight trowel so that you can bury your waste 6 to 8 inches deep. Carry a plastic bag to pack out used toilet paper; a little baking soda will absorb any odors. Make sure you relieve yourself at least 300 feet from any surface water or boggy spot.

Remember to abide by the golden rule of backcountry travel: If you pack it in, pack it out!

Leave no trace—put your ear to the ground and listen carefully. Thousands of people coming behind you are thankful for your courtesy and good sense.

Be Prepared

Generally, hiking in the high country around Aspen is safe, but you must exercise caution as well as your legs. I encourage all hikers to verse themselves completely in the science of backcountry travel—it is knowledge worth having and it is easy to acquire.

Some specific advice:

Know the basics of first aid, including how to treat bleeding, bites and stings, and fractures, strains, or sprains. None of these hikes is so remote that help cannot be reached within a short time, but you would be wise to carry and know how to use simple supplies, like over-the-counter pain relievers, bandages, and ointments. Pack a first-aid kit on each excursion.

Familiarize yourself with the symptoms and treatment of altitude sickness (especially if you are visiting the area from a significantly lesser altitude). If you or one of your party exhibits any symptom of this potentially fatal condition, including headache, nausea, or unusual fatigue, descend to a lower elevation and seek medical attention.

Know the symptoms of both cold- and heat-related conditions, including hypothermia and heatstroke. The best way to avoid these afflictions is to wear appropriate clothing, drink lots of water, eat enough to keep the internal fires properly stoked, and keep a pace that is within your physical limits.

The sun at high altitudes (Aspen sits at more than 7,900 feet) can be brutal, so wear a strong sunscreen.

Afternoon and evening thunderstorms, while rare, harbor a host of potential hazards, including rain, hail, and lightning. Retreat to the safety of the car or other shelter if you suspect the weather will turn, and carry protective clothing.

Keep children under careful watch. Waterways move deceptively fast, animals and plants may harbor danger, and rocky terrain and cliffs are potential hazards. Children should carry a plastic whistle; if they become lost, they should stay in one place and blow the whistle to summon help.

Mountain lions and bears inhabit this wilderness, but encounters are infrequent—the animals tend to avoid humans much as humans like to avoid them. Forest Service rangers can instruct you in proper defensive techniques should you encounter an Aspen beastie.

You will enjoy each of these hikes much more if you wear good socks and hiking boots. Carry a comfortable backpack loaded with water, snacks, and extra clothing, including a warm hat, gloves, and a jacket, and the appropriate maps. Pack a camera, binoculars, or a good novel to curl up with on a warm rock—or any other item that will heighten your enjoyment of these hikes.

1
HARDSCRABBLE AND WILLIAMS LAKES

Type of hike: Out-and-back.
Total distance: 4 miles.
Elevation change: 815 feet.
Maps: USGS Capitol Peak, Crested Butte and Gunnison Recreation Topo Map by Latitude 40.
Jurisdiction: Maroon Bells-Snowmass Wilderness, White River National Forest.
Special considerations: Though the drive to the trailhead is absolutely beautiful, it is also most comfortably made in a four-wheel drive vehicle. If you plan to access this hike in a two-wheel drive car or truck, be prepared to stop at the public parking area and hike west up the rough gravel road to the Hell Roaring Trailhead, adding about 5.6 miles round-trip to the hike (and, unfortunately, moving it out of the easy category, though it is still one of the best in the area). Some hardy and experienced drivers manage to get their two-wheel drive vehicles to either the Capitol Creek Trailhead or the Hell Roaring Trailhead proper, but this is not recommended.

A couple more considerations: Be wary of the weather. This lake is exposed and at treeline; you risk being hit by lightning if a thunderstorm blows in. The significant elevation—Williams Lake is at 10,815 feet—also warrants special care to avoid altitude sickness.

Hardscrabble and Williams Lakes

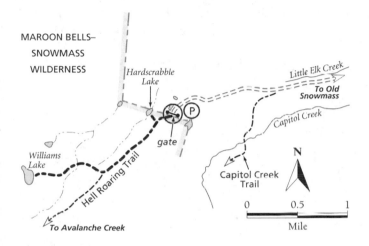

Finding the trailhead: From Aspen, follow Colorado Highway 82 northwest for about 14 miles to Snowmass Road in Old Snowmass. Turn left (southwest) on Snowmass Road and drive 1.6 scenic miles to Capitol Creek Road. Go right (southwest) on Capitol Creek Road. At 6.3 miles, the pavement ends; the gravel road is suitable for two-wheel drive cars. At 7.7 miles, you arrive at a public parking area and the end of the line for most two-wheel drive cars. Continue up the four-wheel-drive road, passing the Capitol Creek Trailhead at 9.5 miles. You will reach the end of the road, a parking area, and the Hell Roaring Trailhead at 10.8 miles.

Key points:
0.0 Trailhead.
0.5 Reach the junction with trail to Hardscrabble Lake.
0.7 Return to the main trail and continue up toward Williams Lake.
1.5 Reach the Williams Lake Trail intersection.
2.0 Arrive at Williams Lake.

The hike: The compelling nature of high mountains most often reveals itself when the forest cloak falls away. Such is the case with Williams Lake, which rests near treeline in the crook of an arm of the rugged Elk Mountains. Hidden by subalpine forest until you step onto the lakeshore, the tarn's stark, sun-washed, rockbound setting is the stuff that draws hikers back to the high country again and again.

This is also the kind of trail that defines what hikers are made of. While not difficult, it is without doubt the most remote of the hikes in this guide, and one of the more challenging. Be prepared to spend the better part of a morning (or day, if you take your time) exploring the trail between Hardscrabble and Williams lakes.

The trail takes off from the trailhead to the southwest, with the barren ridges of Haystack Mountain dominating the southern vistas. Pass through a gate and follow the red soils through the aspen for about 0.2 mile to a small, no-name pond, which is slowly being consumed by meadow. The trail skirts the pond on its left (south) side.

Beyond the pond, the trail climbs into the woods. It appears that trails diverge here; stay left on the lower track (the upper track peters out in deadfall, though you can drop back onto the main route beyond this obstacle). Continue up through the forest to the sign for Hardscrabble Lake at 0.5 mile. Turn right (north) on the path, climbing up and over the wooded lip of the basin that holds this perfectly oval, bottle-green lake. On a peaceful day, it is hard to imagine how the lake got the name "Hardscrabble"—or how, for that matter, the trail earned its Hell Roaring moniker. Perhaps the explorer that dubbed them both was unlucky enough to arrive in the dead of winter, struggling up the trail through fierce winds to an ice-locked and unfriendly lake. Then again, the names could have been the work of a grouchy cartographer…

Hardscrabble Lake might be the end of the road if you have hiked from the two-wheel drive parking lot. But if you have more juice, or if you started from the Hell Roaring Trailhead with Williams Lake in your sights, return to the main trail at 0.7 mile and turn right (southwest). Steep climbing through the mixed evergreen forest leads to a sweeping turn at the edge of an aspen grove, where you can peer down into the steep Capitol Creek defile, and enjoy views of the Haystack and Christiana massifs.

The ascent continues as a series of steep pitches broken by relatively moderate grades on the heavily forested ridgeline. The Williams Lake Trail intersection is at about 1.5 miles, at the base of a downhill pitch. Go right (northwest) on the path to Williams Lake, which descends steeply into a moist shady hollow.

Raised bridges lead you through a swampy stretch, which may be particularly bug-laden in July, but also boasts a wonderful wildflower display. A formal bridge leads over the braided stream, which is swollen with snowmelt early in the season, and a red-bottomed trickle by August.

The climb up and out of the boggy hollow is again steep, and traces the path of a small but noisy stream swaddled in greenery. The trail flattens in a jumbled woodland and sidles alongside the little waterway, climbs over a ridge, then descends to another footbridge. Another climb leads to a series of bridges before you make the final ascent to Williams Lake, which is at 2 miles.

Find a nice place to relax and contemplate the spacious but shallow tarn, cradled in a red-rock cirque at treeline, before you return via the same route.

Option: If you want to make this trail part of a long shuttle hike or a backpacking trip, continue southwest on the Hell Roaring Trail past the Williams Lake turnoff; this will take you up over the Elk Mountains and drop you onto the Avalanche Creek Trail, in the shadow of snow-crowned Mount Sopris.

2
HIGHLINE TRAIL

Type of hike: Out-and-back.
Total distance: 2 miles.
Elevation change: 520 feet.
Maps: USGS Highland Peak; Snowmass Village Summer Trail Map for Hikers and Bikers.
Jurisdiction: Snowmass Village.

Finding the trailhead: To reach the northernmost trailhead from the roundabout, take Colorado Highway 82 northwest for about 5 miles to Brush Creek Road at Snowmass Village. Turn left (west), and follow Brush Creek Road up the valley to Highline Road. Turn left (south) on Highline Road, and go 0.1 mile to the trailhead, which is on the left (east) side of the road. Extremely limited parking is available alongside Highline Road near the trailhead.

If you do not mind carving off a short section of the trail, you can drive up Highline Road to Cemetery Lane. Go left (southeast) on Cemetery Lane and park alongside the gravel road near the trail crossing; there is room for two or three cars to park here. You can also park in the small lot for the Snowmass Village Community Cemetery, which is located about 0.2 mile farther (southeast) on Cemetery Lane.

Highline Trail

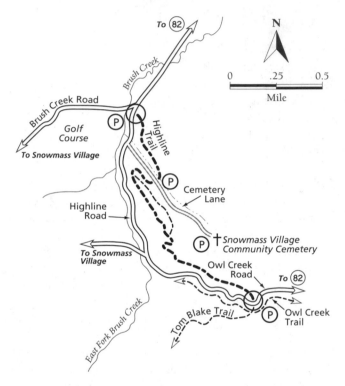

To reach the Owl Creek Trailhead, at the east end of the trail, from Brush Creek Road, go 1.1 miles south on Highline Road to its intersection with Owl Creek Road. Turn left (east) on Owl Creek Road, and go 0.4 mile to the parking area, which is on the right (south) side.

Key points:
0.0 Trailhead.
0.3 Drop into Hidden Valley and cross Cemetery Lane.
0.5 Reach the trail intersection in the saddle.
1.0 Arrive at Owl Creek Road.

The hike: Traversing a hillside overlooking the Snowmass Valley, the Highline Trail is a pleasant romp through the fragrant scrubland that covers the Roaring Fork Valley at lower elevations. Most pleasant either in the morning, before the day grows too warm, or in the late afternoon, when the settling sun paints the mountains pink and orange, this trail sees little traffic, and offers a pleasant alternative to the evergreen forests that shade most of the area's hiking trails. The trail is described here from the Highline Road trailhead to Owl Creek Road, but can be hiked in either direction.

Beginning on Highline Road, the path climbs away from the pavement quickly, launching into the scrub oak, sage, and wildflowers that cover the hillside. After a rolling traverse that gradually leads you east and away from Highline Road, you drop into Hidden Valley. The copse of aspen at the eastern end of the valley shades the picturesque Snowmass Village Community Cemetery.

At 0.3 mile, the path crosses Cemetery Lane. Once across the road, the narrow singletrack traces a ram-shackle fence, then climbs to an overlook of Snowmass Village, the golf course, and the ski mountain, with Capitol Peak and its neighbors rising to the southwest.

Stay left on the upper path, avoiding the ramp-like spur on the right, and keep climbing.

Switchbacks swirl you up onto the ridgetop, and the trail's pitch eases, though you keep climbing. A withered-looking side trail breaks off to the left; stay right on the main path. Another steep pitch peaks on top of a knob, where a wide spot in the trail serves as yet another overlook.

Drop into a saddle and to a trail intersection at about 0.5 mile. The Highline Trail continues to the right (south); the left trail drops back down into Hidden Valley before curving back to meet the main path, and can serve as an alternative route on the return trip.

The Highline Trail bends southeast, arcing around the knoll and sporting awesome views. Near trail's end, Owl Creek Road comes into view. The route passes behind the Snowmass Operations Facility and drops to Owl Creek Road at 1 mile. Return as you came.

Options: To hike farther, cross Owl Creek Road and pick up the paved Owl Creek Trail, a popular cycling route that heads west through lovely ranch lands and ends at Colorado 82. Or, take a side trip to the graveyard at the head of Hidden Valley, where you will find a poignant handful of graves set amid tall grass, flowers, and old-growth aspen. This will add 0.4 mile to your hike. You can also vary your return trip by taking the right-hand trail at the saddle; this drops into Hidden Valley and traverses the north-facing slope before rejoining the main trail just above the switchbacks.

3
EAST SNOWMASS CREEK OVERLOOK TRAIL

Type of hike: Loop.
Total distance: 1.5 miles (including the walk between lifts).
Elevation change: 320 feet.
Maps: USGS Highland Peak; Snowmass Village Summer Trail Map for Hikers and Bikers.
Jurisdiction: Snowmass Village.

Finding the trailhead: Take Colorado Highway 82 northwest for about 5 miles to Brush Creek Road at Snowmass Village. Turn left (west), and follow Brush Creek Road for about 5.2 miles up the valley, passing the golf course, shopping center, and numerous condominiums, to its intersection with Divide Road. Bear left, switchbacking eastward, to Snowmelt Road, which serves Snowmass Village Mall. Park in any of the lots, then cross the road and walk through the village to the lift ticket kiosk, where lift tickets can be purchased daily. Lifts operate between 9:30 A.M. and 4 P.M. Ride the Burlingame Lift to its end, then follow the Village Bound Trail to the right (west) for about 0.5 mile to the Sam's Knob Lift. Ride this lift to its terminus atop the knob at 10,630 feet. Drop south over the knob on the footpath to the service road, turn right (south), then quickly right again onto the signed trail.

East Snowmass Creek Overlook Trail

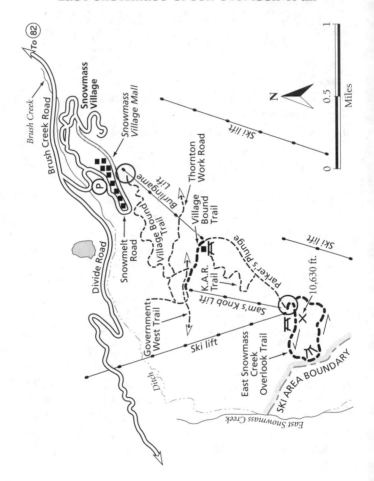

Key points:
0.0 Trailhead.
0.8 Reach the East Snowmass Creek Overlook.
1.0 Return to the Sam's Knob Lift.

The hike: Nearly every ski resort in Colorado has developed hiking and mountain biking trails on its slopes—a summertime lure for visitors. Riding the lifts to the trails opens wonderful worlds to families, to those who are short on time but have a hankering for a high-country jaunt, and to skiers who want to ride a lift in August or scope the contours of the mountain without its blanket of wintertime snow.

The East Snowmass Creek Overlook Trail is one of the few hiking-only trails accessed via lifts at the Snowmass Ski Area. It winds around Sam's Knob to a stunning vista point overlooking the steep canyon carved by East Snowmass Creek. The path is lined with interpretive markers, but guides were not available when this trail was researched. Check at the lift ticket office or Snowmass Village Mall information office to see if a guide is available when you visit.

To reach the trailhead proper from the top of the Sam's Knob Lift, walk south down the backside of the knob to the service road. Go right (south), then quickly right again (west) onto the signed trail. Cross through a gully and pass marker 3 before entering the subalpine fir forest.

The trail drops into a rocky gully, then passes markers 5, 6, and 7 in a flower-strewn meadow watered by a small pond. The trail begins to climb into the woods above the meadow, passing markers 8 and 9, and following trail signs across the service road. Beyond, the trail climbs steadily and steeply through the woods to marker 10.

By the time you reach markers 12 and 13, the woodland has begun to thin. A final curve, and you will find yourself perched on a ridgetop with a fantastic overview of the East Snowmass Creek canyon at about 0.8 mile. The steep-walled creek chasm climbs southeast into the Maroon Bells–Snowmass Wilderness and toward the high peaks of the Elk Range, which shed their deep green forest skirts to expose steep, dusky, barren heights punctuated by snowfields that linger into late summer.

From the overlook, the trail curves left (northeast), tracing the ridge as it traverses back into the forest. The roller coaster path courses through the woods to a ski slope at the ski area boundary, then heads down toward a service road (a sign labeled Sam's Knob indicates the correct route). Views south and east through the Maroon Bells–Snowmass Wilderness, home to many of Colorado's fourteen-thousand foot peaks, accompany your descent.

The gravel road loops left (northwest) back to the Sam's Knob Lift at about the 1-mile mark. Ride the lift back to the Snowmass Village Mall and the trailhead, or chose one of the options below.

Option: No need to ride the lift back to the trailhead if you have a hankering to continue hiking—especially since it is

all downhill from here. Two hikers-only trails lead down
to the Village Bound Trail, the main route back to the village mall. Begin your descent by following the service
road around the base of the lift knob to Parker's Plunge,
and head down Banzai Ridge—down! down!—to the
Coney Glade Lift. Dive behind the lift to the K.A.R.
Trail, which breaks off to the left (west) and leads down
switchbacks through meadow and fir forest to the top of
the Burlingame Lift. Hiking-only options end here, but
all trails lead down: choose the Village Bound Trail, the
Luge Trail, or the Burlingame Trail for the final portion
of the descent. This will add up to 3 miles and about
2,000 feet of elevation loss to your hike.

4
SNOWMASS VILLAGE NATURE TRAIL

Type of hike: Loop.
Total distance: 2 miles.
Elevation change: 240 feet.
Maps: USGS Highland Peak; Snowmass Village Summer Trail Map for Hikers and Bikers.
Jurisdiction: Snowmass Village.

Finding the trailhead: Take Colorado Highway 82 northwest for about 5 miles to Brush Creek Road at Snowmass Village. Turn left (west), and follow Brush Creek Road for about 5.2 miles up the valley, passing the golf course, the shopping center, and numerous condominiums, to its intersection with Divide Road. Bear left, switchbacking eastward, to Snowmelt Road, which serves Snowmass Village Mall. The trailhead is on the right (west) opposite the Elbert Lane entrance to the village mall. Park in any of the village parking lots opposite Snowmass Village Mall; lot 8 is convenient. No facilities are available at the trailhead proper, but food, restrooms, clothing, and other amenities can be found in Snowmass Village.

Key points:
0.0 Trailhead.
0.4 Check out the miner's cabin and picnic area.

Snowmass Village Nature Trail

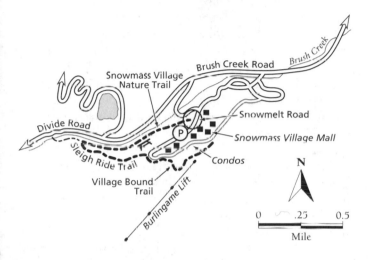

1.0 Turn left (east) onto the Sleigh Ride Trail.
2.0 Reach Snowmass Village.

The hike: This gentle little trail loop has "take the kids" written all over it. Meandering easily up toward Divide Road and the high country west of Snowmass Village, the hike offers up wildflowers to identify, the ruins of a miner's cabin to explore, and a creek to splash in. Anyone with a hankering for wilderness on a small-scale will enjoy this jaunt.

Depending on where you park, the trail may begin by descending stairs from the lots to the trailhead, which is wedged between Snowmelt Road and Lot 8. The narrow track hovers above the road, on a slope covered with a thick undergrowth and shaded by aspen. Pass a sign acknowledging the work of the Rotary Club of Snowmass Village, which maintains the trail, and continue west on the path.

Cross a culvert at about 0.2 mile, and at 0.3 mile, cross a small slide path and pass a narrow footpath that leads right (northwest) to the creek that flows alongside the nature trail. The aspen groves through which you pass—as with all aspen groves in the Snowmass area—put on a spectacular show when the leaves turn in autumn.

Reach a nice shady spot in a glade of fir trees. The trail spans a culvert, then borders the willows that shroud the banks of the noisy creek. Another footpath branches right to where the creek rumbles through rocks and fallen logs, then arcs back to the main trail.

At 0.4 mile, a narrow footpath breaks from the main route, bearing right (north). Take this path, which crosses a little footbridge into a small meadow and threads through a marshy area. Boards have been placed along the trail to keep your feet dry. The path leads to a decrepit miner's cabin tucked under a tree.

When your explorations at the cabin are complete, return to the main route, and continue west, passing a small picnic area with great views down the Brush Creek valley. The trail passes through alternating meadows and small glades of fir and aspen as it continues its gentle ascent. At about 0.8 mile, Divide Road comes into view to the right (north), with the creek providing more than ample noise coverage for any auto traffic on the little-traveled route. Yet another footpath branches to the creek, where a split log bridge spans the waterway and offers access to the road. A small grassy area alongside the brook is a nice place to rest.

The route continues west, ascending through more meadows and aspen, to a final, short up that deposits you at the intersection with the Sleigh Ride Trail at 1 mile. Divide Road is another 0.1 mile to the right (west). To get back to the trailhead, turn left (east) on the Sleigh Ride Trail.

The path is broad enough to be easily shared by all trail users, and descends so gently you will think it is flat. After about 0.25 mile, the trail passes beneath massive homes that dot the mountainside to the right (south). Wonderful views open east down the Brush Creek valley.

At about 1.5 miles, the trail collides with the Top of the Village condominium complex. Go right on the dirt road, staying straight (east) at the road junctions that follow, for about 0.1 mile, to the foot of a ski run and a triple chairlift. A bench marks the spot where the Village Bound Trail takes off to the left (northeast). Take the Village Bound Trail, which drops through aspens to another ski run, then zigzags down to the chairlift and the village. Go left (west) into the mall at 2 miles, and pass by all the eateries to Snowmelt Road and the Snowmass Village Nature Trailhead.

Option: If you want to avoid potential mountain bike traffic, you can return to the trailhead via the nature trail. Biking on this trail is prohibited between 8 A.M. and 5 P.M.

Rio Grande Trail West
Sunnyside Trail

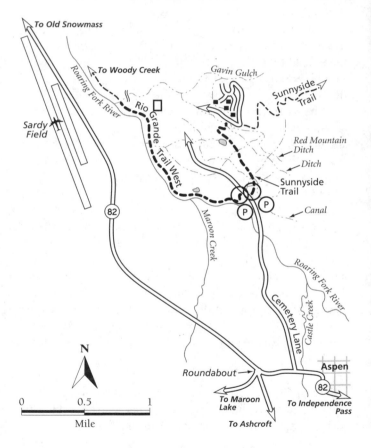

To Old Snowmass

To Woody Creek

Gavin Gulch

Sunnyside Trail

Roaring Fork River

Rio Grande Trail West

Sardy Field

Red Mountain Ditch

Ditch

Sunnyside Trail

P   P

Canal

82

Maroon Creek

Roaring Fork River

Cemetery Lane

Castle Creek

N

Roundabout

Aspen

82

0   0.5   1

Mile

To Maroon Lake

To Ashcroft

To Independence Pass

5
RIO GRANDE TRAIL WEST

Type of hike: Out-and-back.
Total distance: 2.6 miles.
Elevation change: 80 feet.
Maps: USGS Aspen; National Geographic/Trails
Illustrated Aspen and Independence Pass; Aspen, Crested
Butte and Gunnison Recreation Topo Map by Latitude 40.
Jurisdiction: White River National Forest.

Finding the trailhead: From the roundabout, take Colorado
Highway 82 east for about 0.25 mile to Cemetery Lane.
Turn left (north) and follow Cemetery Lane for 1.2 miles
down to the parking area at Henry Stein Park.

Key points:
0.0 Trailhead.
0.5 Pass beneath the grotto.
0.8 Pass the pond.
1.0 Hike onto the treeless flat above the river.
1.3 Reach the trailside waterfalls.

The hike: The volatile Roaring Fork River dominates the
first part of this easy, relatively flat hike, thundering
through a gray-rock canyon where whitewater rushes past
sun-baked rocks and feeds cool, inviting pools. As the trail
climbs away from the river, the environment becomes arid.

Scrub clings to the hillsides above the wide track; the air gets noticeably hotter; and the cyclists that share the trail with hikers get grumpier. Then, around the proverbial next bend, water appears to bleed from the rock overhanging the route. Cascading gently into a pool alongside the trail, and streaking the hillside with mineral color and lichen, the little waterfall makes for a delightful turnaround point.

Begin the hike by heading right (west) down the trail, passing through a thick evergreen grove into a canyon overgrown with cottonwood and box elder. Faint angler's trails lead down to the Roaring Fork. The trail passes into a mini-gorge; if you are lucky, you may spot climbers on the steep rock formation on the right (north) side of the trail.

At the 0.5-mile mark, you will pass beneath an overhanging grotto, which catches the sounds of the river and flings them back into the rich riparian growth along the shoreline. Beyond, naked gray cliffs frame the southwest side of the river, which dumps over small falls. A placid pond is on the opposite (right/northeast) side of the trail at 0.8 mile.

The trail ascends beyond the Maroon Creek confluence and picnic spot on the left (southwest). Hike onto an arid, treeless flat above the river at the 1-mile mark, passing a road that leads left (southwest) and down to the river. A bridge spans the stream below. Continue straight and up (northwest).

At about 1.3 miles, you pass an overgrown ravine, then reach the trailside waterfalls. Several streams spill down the multi-colored cliff into the clear pool below. This hike ends here, but the trail continues up onto the plain above, where views open of the Roaring Fork river valley. If you choose to stop at the waterfalls, return as you came.

Options: Beyond the falls, the Rio Grande Trail climbs through alpine desert toward Woody Creek, topping out on a broad, scrubby plain that stretches down the Roaring Fork Valley. You can walk for miles on this arid flat. Between Woody Creek and Old Snowmass, the Rio Grande Trail is paved and popular with bicyclists. If you head in the other direction, you can connect this section of trail with the Rio Grande Trail East (Hike 7), which follows the Roaring Fork River through downtown Aspen.

6
SUNNYSIDE TRAIL

see map page 28

Type of hike: Out-and-back.
Total distance: Approximately 2 miles.
Elevation change: 680 feet.
Maps: USGS Aspen; National Geographic/Trails Illustrated Aspen and Independence Pass; Aspen, Crested Butte and Gunnison Recreation Topo Map by Latitude 40.
Trail number: 1987.
Jurisdiction: White River National Forest.

Finding the trailhead: From the roundabout, take Colorado Highway 82 east for about 0.25 mile to Cemetery Lane. Turn left (north) and follow Cemetery Lane for 1.5 miles to the small parking area on the left (southeast) side of the road. The trailhead is across the road from the lot.

Key points:
0.0 Trailhead.
0.5 Reach the S-curves.
1.0 Arrive at the bench by the last ditch.

The hike: Up and up and up—the Sunnyside Trail climbs relentlessly across the scrub-covered south-facing slopes of Red Mountain. It is a workout, but the views give the climb a substantial charm. Look northwest, where the Roaring Fork Valley broadens and grows rounder as it

32

drops toward the Colorado River basin. Look east past the steep green slopes of Aspen Ski Mountain to the steely peaks that guard Independence Pass. And gaze southwest at the pink and purple summits of the Maroon Bells and Pyramid Peak, which, at more than 14,000 feet, tower over the valley.

You can hike from Sunnyside into the Hunter Creek drainage, an effort that will take the better part of a day. The hike described here leads to the last ditch (which is by no means a comment on the hiker's efforts).

To begin, climb past the information sign, cross the ditch, and enjoy the shade while it lasts. The trail levels at the second ditch, and a trail sign marks the way at an otherwise unmarked trail intersection. Go up and right (east), around two switchbacks, past a second trail sign and through a fence.

The trail traverses three gullies, and flattens briefly before swinging upward in broad S-curves at about 0.5 mile. Pass beneath large boulders, then climb steeply again, around a trailside boulder, through some scrub oak, and over a pipe. Sardy Field, the Aspen/Pitkin County airport, dominates the southern vistas as the path continues west across the mountainside.

A lonely juniper—a refreshing patch of greenery on the parched, exposed slope—crowds the trail as you climb on. The trail switches back yet again at about 0.8 mile, offering views southeast of the area ski mountains. Cross a ditch, pass a gate, and keep climbing. You will pass beneath a home with stunning views of the Maroon Bells; beyond, the trail roller coasters amid jumbles of rock and scrub. Negotiate yet another switchback, and gaze up at yet another fabulous home. The last ditch is just beyond this second home, at about 1 mile.

A ditch-side seat offers great 180-degree views, and a cooling burst of vegetation. The trail carries on, crossing a private drive and continuing a dry ascent, but this is the end of the short-hike line. Retrace your steps to the trailhead (2 miles).

Option: If you want to take on a 10-mile one-way adventure, you can continue upward on the Sunnyside Trail, which eventually meets the Hunter Creek Trail, and follow Hunter Creek back into Aspen—a vigorous hike that will take you the better part of a day to complete. Carry a topographic map to help you with route-finding. If you do not want to take on such an energetic endeavor, but want more than what has been described here, simply continue on the trail until you're satisfied, then turn around and hike back down.

7
RIO GRANDE TRAIL EAST

Type of hike: Out-and-back.
Total distance: Approximately 5 miles.
Elevation change: 40 feet.
Maps: USGS Aspen; National Geographic/Trails Illustrated Aspen and Independence Pass; Aspen, Crested Butte and Gunnison Recreation Topo Map by Latitude 40.
Jurisdiction: City of Aspen.

Finding the trailhead: From the roundabout, continue east through downtown Aspen, following Colorado 82 (Main Street) to Neale Street. Turn left (north) on Neale, and follow it to Herron Park. The paved path begins in Herron Park. Parking is available at the trailhead, along with benches, restrooms, and a tot lot. A portion of the trail is paved and accessible to persons with disabilities.

Key points:
0.0 Trailhead.
0.5 Pass under Mill Street.
0.7 Cross a bridge; the trail surface changes from concrete to asphalt.
1.7 Reach the Grundley Bridge.
2.5 Arrive at the Aspen Institute.

The hike: Cradled in the bottomlands along the Roaring

Rio Grande Trail East

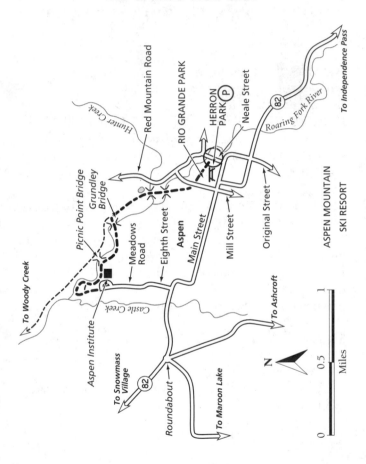

Fork River, the paved Rio Grande Trail cuts through the heart of downtown Aspen. It is the perfect choice for families with small children, for those who want to stretch their legs between a continental breakfast and a gourmet lunch, or for those who need to unwind after work. Easy, lovely, and extremely popular, this stretch of domesticated wilderness is a classic compliment to Aspen's glitter and bustle.

To begin, stroll through Herron Park, with its friendly riverside beach, to a boardwalk and bridge that span the Roaring Fork River. At the intersection of the Rio Grande Trail and the spur to Oklahoma Flats, stay left (northwest) along the main trail, passing Newberry Park. The trail forks again at Rio Grande Road, with a dirt track breaking off to the right (riverside). Stay left, on the pavement.

As it heads into Rio Grande Park, the path loops by a pond, skate park, soccer field, and the stage of Aspen's Theatre In The Park. At the next trail fork, signed for the Aspen Art Museum, stay left, crossing the trestle bridge (Ron Krajian Bridge). Pass beneath Mill Street at about 0.5 mile, and stay left at the next trail fork, winding past one of many dedicated benches to a four-way intersection with spur trails.

Stay to the right on the main path, walking over the bridge and passing a pond on the left (south) side of the trail. Cross a driveway and continue on the concrete track to yet another bridge at about 0.7 mile; a sign noting mileage indicates that distances have been measured along this portion of the route. The trail surface becomes asphalt, and passes homes screened by aspens.

By the quarter-mile marker (about 1.2 miles), the trail has left the downtown area and presses close to the river, wedged between the watercourse and private homes. You share the trail with cyclists, so stay to the right. A couple of curves lead down to the 0.5-mile marker (1.7 miles); the Grundley Bridge is about 100 yards beyond.

You can turn around here, or continue northwest on the paved Rio Grande Trail, or take a path that edges to the wild side, which is described here. A footpath, marked by a bench and trash can, leads down to the bridge. Cross the Roaring Fork, and turn right (northwest), toward the Meadows and the Aspen Institute.

This lovely little trail, on which bikes are prohibited, leads down, then up to a Y-intersection. The left fork leads to the Aspen Institute; stay right, heading toward the Meadows. Follow the edge of the bluff above the river, then drop down into the shade at riverside.

Reach another trail intersection at about 2 miles. Again, stay right (riverside), passing over a small footbridge. Small paths branch right to the river; stay left (northwest), passing through meadowland. Pass signs for Picnic Point Bridge; if you go right (northeast), you will climb over the bridge and back onto the Rio Grande Trail.

Instead, head toward Aspen, bearing left (west) and up onto the lollipop-loop that winds through the Meadows. Stay to the right, on the lower trail, following the signs. The trail widens to a wildflower-lined doubletrack, which ends with a steep climb onto the beautiful grounds of the Aspen Institute at about 2.5 miles. Return as you came.

Options: If you want to vary your route back to the trail-head, you can take the Picnic Point Bridge back to the Rio Grande Trail and retrace your steps to the Herron Park trailhead from there. Or, if you plan ahead, you can have someone pick you up at the Aspen Institute. But I suggest you circle back to the trailhead via the back streets of Aspen. A trail leads south to Eighth Street, westernmost on the Aspen street grid. From Eighth, turn left (east) and follow the street of your choice—Hallam, Smuggler, Francis, Main, or some combination of these—back toward the east portion of town. Neale Street branches off Original Street, which intersects Main Street/CO 82.

8
UTE TRAIL

Type of hike: Out-and-back.
Total distance: Approximately 2 miles.
Elevation change: 1,160 feet.
Maps: USGS Aspen; National Geographic/Trails Illustrated Aspen and Independence Pass; Aspen, Crested Butte and Gunnison Recreation Topo Map by Latitude 40.
Jurisdiction: City of Aspen.

Finding the trailhead: From the roundabout, continue east through downtown Aspen, following Colorado Highway 82 (Main Street) to Original Street. Follow Original south (right) for 0.3 mile to Ute Avenue. Bear left (east) on Ute for 0.4 mile to Ute Park. The trailhead is opposite the park.

Key points:
0.0 Trailhead.
1.0 Round the 19th switchback and enjoy the views.

The hike: If you want to break a sweat, this is the hike for you. If you are weak in the knees, move on.

The Ute Trail is a hardy hiker's hike—straight up through dense forest to a rock outcrop that offers a stunning eagle's-eye view of the countryside. Below lies Aspen, laid out like a checkerboard on the floor of the valley. Eastward rise the steep mountains surrounding

Ute Trail

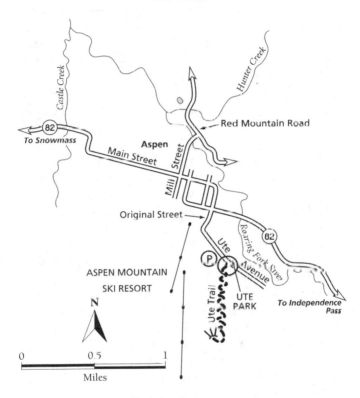

Independence Pass. Mount Sopris, portal of the Roaring Fork Valley, towers to the west, a solitary symmetrical peak of astounding simplicity and beauty.

The path to the overlook is a difficult one, strewn with switchbacks (19 total—count 'em) and broken into alternating forested sections and sections denuded by ava-lanches. The trail borders Aspen Ski Mountain, which is notorious for its steeps; after this hike, you will know why.

Begin the hike by skirting a private drive, then plunge past small aspen around the first switchback. Three more switchbacks lead through short, dense shrubbery; by the fourth switchback you have entered the evergreens. The fifth and sixth switchbacks climb the wide apron of an avalanche slide path. The trail dips before the eighth switchback, then climbs across an avalanche chute.

The path drops into a gully and climbs steeply out again, then you emerge from the forest onto the narrow-ing avalanche slope and the ninth switchback. Flat spots lie between the next three switchbacks. At the twelfth, you again look into the maw of the avalanche chute.

The thirteenth switchback offers views up the valley, as does the fifteenth. Climb over an exposed root, and ping-pong through the final switchbacks. Beyond, the path crosses the top of the avalanche path. Climb over a jumble of roots and deadfall; the trail traverses a bit farther, then leaves the trees at the orange rock outcrop that serves as the eagle's perch at about the 1-mile mark.

After you have enjoyed the stellar views, plummet to the trailhead. Keep in mind that hiking downhill can be murder on the knees and hips, so hike with care.

9
HUNTER CREEK TRAIL

Type of hike: Out-and-back.
Total distance: Approximately 3 miles.
Elevation change: 440 feet.
Maps: USGS Aspen; National Geographic/Trails Illustrated Aspen and Independence Pass; Aspen, Crested Butte and Gunnison Recreation Topo Map by Latitude 40.
Trail number: 2194.
Jurisdiction: White River National Forest.

Finding the trailhead: From the roundabout, follow Colorado Highway 82 east into Aspen, where it doubles as Main Street, to its intersection with Mill Street. Turn left (north) on Mill Street, and drive 0.3 mile to Red Mountain Road. Follow Red Mountain Road for 0.1 mile to Lone Pine Road and turn right (east). The trailhead, with some on-street parking, is 0.1 mile up Lone Pine Road, on the left (north). This trail is very popular, so parking may be limited. The signed trail begins behind the condominium complex.

Key points:
0.0 Trailhead.
1.0 Reach the river-cobble staircase and bridge.
1.5 Reach the paved road.

Hunter Creek Trail

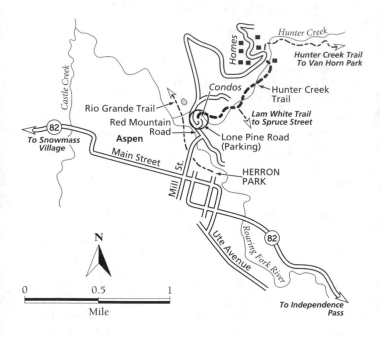

The hike: Rollicking Hunter Creek is the centerpiece of this hike. The path runs through dense riparian forest near the creek's confluence with the Roaring Fork; as the trail gets steeper and more invigorating, so does the creek, splashing joyfully under scenic bridges and over polished rocks. Pick any bridge along the route as a rest stop; each also offers a perfect turning point.

This description only covers the lower portion of the trail, which continues beyond the bridges for many miles into the Hunter-Fryingpan Wilderness, offering access to Van Horn Park and the McNamara Hut, a popular destination for backcountry skiers.

To begin, walk past the condos into the riparian zone. Pass the trail sign and cross a series of boardwalks and two small bridges. As you proceed, Hunter Creek grows more raucous.

Climb through oversized river cobbles to the first major bridge at about 0.3 mile. The trail continues to climb, and crosses yet another boardwalk, then crosses a bridge over a ditch. At this point you leave the cooling shade of the riparian zone, and the hiking becomes more arid. Despite the change in habitat, Hunter Creek still rumbles along on the right (southeast) side of the path.

Cross the third bridge—Hunter Creek presents itself here as a series of rivulets among boulders that appear to have been jumbled by a much more powerful watercourse. Climb to an intersection with the Lani White Trail, which offers access to Spruce Street. Go left (northeast) and up the stairs, remaining on the Hunter Creek Trail, which is briefly steep, then levels off in an aspen grove.

At about 1 mile, the trail climbs a river-cobble staircase to a rocky terrace above yet another bridge. Drop a quick switchback to the span. This bridge is an ideal place to pause and take in the views, and is a great turnaround point.

Beyond the bridge, the trail continues up and over another boardwalk. Two switchbacks lead above the creek, and the trail grows rockier. Another switchback leads you farther from the creek, which now sports a rusty pipeline. At the trail fork, go right to visit a small diversion dam and spillway; the left fork climbs to a switchback in the paved road above. This is the turnaround point for this short hike (1.5 miles), but you can continue onward and upward for as long as you choose (see Options below). Or, you can return as you came.

Options: The Hunter Creek Trail continues for miles into the Hunter-Fryingpan Wilderness, eventually intersecting a number of other trails, including the Hunter Valley Trail (#1992), the Woody Creek Trail (#1994), and the Midway Creek Trail (#1993). All these options translate into longer loops or shuttle hikes for hikers with the time and energy. Consult a good topographic map for loop options and details.

10
MAROON CREEK TRAIL

Type of hike: Out-and-back or shuttle.
Total distance: 7 miles (3.5 miles with shuttle).
Elevation change: 870 feet.
Maps: USGS Maroon Bells and Highland Peak; National Geographic/Trails Illustrated Maroon Bells, Redstone, Marble; Aspen, Crested Butte and Gunnison Recreation Topo Map by Latitude 40.
Trail number: 1982.
Jurisdiction: Maroon Bells–Snowmass Wilderness, White River National Forest.

Finding the trailhead: The parking lot at Maroon Lake fills early, and can be accessed during the summer only before 8:30 A.M., when the road is open to traffic, or during the snow-free months of spring and autumn. From the roundabout, follow Maroon Creek Road (Colorado Highway 13) southwest for about 10.5 miles to its end at West Maroon Portal. If you start after 8:30 A.M. between mid-June and September, you will have to take the shuttle bus, which runs regularly during the summer. For shuttle schedules, contact the Aspen Ranger District at (970) 925-3445 or visit the Aspen office at 806 West Hallam. Restrooms, picnic facilities, and information are available at the trailhead.

Maroon Creek Trail

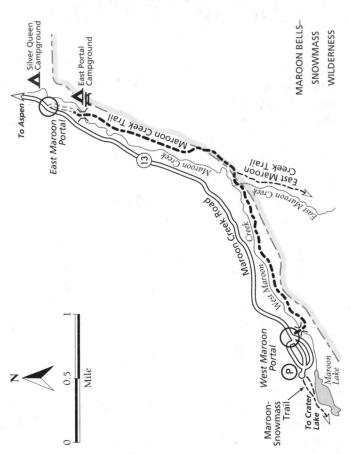

Key points:
0.0 Trailhead.
0.5 Reach the first bridge.
1.5 Arrive at the junction with the East Maroon Creek Trail.
3.5 Reach the picnic grounds at East Maroon Portal.

The hike: Most hikers who have found their way into the Maroon Creek canyon head southwest, touring Maroon Lake or heading into the marvelous wilderness surrounding the Maroon Bells. This trail is the one less traveled, skipping through the flower-covered hillsides above Maroon Creek that you zipped past as you drove or took the shuttle up the canyon, and serving up great views of the steep pink-tinted slopes of the surrounding mountains.

While the scenery and seclusion of the Maroon Creek Trail is marvelous, the trail surface can be some-what treacherous, especially after a rainstorm, when water and horse hooves combine to transform the path into a pock-marked quagmire.

The trail begins at the west end of the day-use parking area, on the shore of West Maroon Creek. Cross the bridge, then turn left (northeast) and follow the trail downstream. The path initially heads down through a mixed fir forest, with the cataracts of West Maroon Creek on the left (northwest), then evolves into a rollicking up-and-down affair with rock stairs and bulkheads at streams that feed the creek. When the forest opens, you can look north at the red pinnacles of Stevens Mountain.

At about 0.2 mile, the trail crosses a talus field overlooking a relatively calm stretch of creek and the overnight parking area. The talus makes for rough walking—good shoes are a must—but the trail is fairly clear. Behind you, the Maroon Bells tower over the valley; the talus field and groves of aspen sweep up the huge slide chute to the right (south), and pikas chirp from their hiding places in the crevices of the jumbled pink rock.

Beyond the talus field, the trail snakes back to the creek and into the forest again. At about 0.5 mile, you will reach the first bridge spanning West Maroon Creek on your left (west), a trail sign, and a switchback. Continue right (northeast) on the main route. The trail conditions deteriorate, hammered by horses, as the creek grows livelier. Pass another footbridge, marked with a sign warning you to keep out. The bridge leads to private residences tucked in the woods on the opposite side of the creek.

The forest opens enough to reveal a broad meadow that stretches away to the north, then breaks up into a meadow itself at about 1 mile. You have great views down the valley from this meadow, and the small meadows that follow, which are intermingled with a grand old stand of aspen, and smaller stands of trees and stumps. Maroon Creek drops into a red-rock canyon before the trail rounds a grassy knob and drops to a bridge over the rapids of East Maroon Creek. To the right (south), the canyon wall yawns open, and both East Maroon Creek and the East Maroon Creek Trail tumble out.

The East Maroon Creek Trail intersects the Maroon

Creek Trail at 1.5 miles. To reach the junction, cross marshy areas around the confluence of the two vigorous Maroon Creeks on elevated platforms, then climb steeply through aspen to the trail crossing.

Turn left (northeast and down the valley) on the Maroon Creek Trail, enjoying great views from the open hillside into which the trail is cut. The path steadily but easily descends through alternating meadows and aspen groves. In spring and early summer, the meadows are thick with wildflowers; as the season edges toward autumn, the flowers change from purples, pinks, and reds of penstemon, wild rose, and indian paintbrush to the yellows and whites of asters and yarrow, and are finally overshadowed in late September and early October by the fiery oranges and golds of the aspen.

As you near the trail's end at East Maroon Portal, the trail flattens in a meadow, then wanders into the East Maroon Portal picnic area and campground at 3.5 miles. You can either hike back up the canyon to West Maroon Portal, meet your ride in the ample East Maroon Portal parking area, or hike up to Maroon Creek Road to catch a shuttle back to the trailhead.

Maroon Lake Scenic Trail
Crater Lake

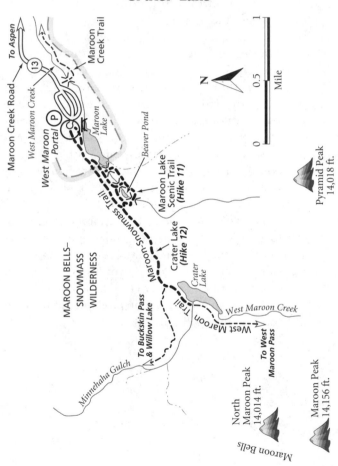

To Aspen

Maroon Creek Road

(13)

Maroon Creek Trail

West Maroon Creek

West Maroon Portal

P

Maroon Lake

Beaver Pond

N

0.5   1

Mile

0

Snowmass Trail

Maroon Lake Scenic Trail (Hike 11)

MAROON BELLS–SNOWMASS WILDERNESS

Pyramid Peak 14,018 ft.

Crater Lake (Hike 12)

Maroon–Snowmass Trail

Crater Lake

West Maroon Creek

West Maroon Trail

To Buckskin Pass & Willow Lake

To West Maroon Pass

Minnehaha Gulch

North Maroon Peak 14,014 ft.

Maroon Peak 14,156 ft.

Maroon Bells

11
MAROON LAKE
SCENIC TRAIL

Type of hike: Loop.
Total distance: 2 miles.
Elevation change: 120 feet.
Maps: USGS Maroon Bells; National Geographic/Trails Illustrated Maroon Bells, Redstone, Marble; Aspen, Crested Butte and Gunnison Recreation Topo Map by Latitude 40.
Jurisdiction: Maroon Bells Snowmass Wilderness, White River National Forest.

Finding the trailhead: The limited parking that is available at Maroon Lake can be accessed during the summer only before 8:30 A.M., when the road is open to traffic, or anytime during the snow-free months of spring and autumn. From the roundabout, follow Maroon Creek Road (Colorado Highway 13) southwest for about 10.5 miles to its end at West Maroon Portal. If you start after 8:30 A.M. between mid-June and September, you will have to take the shuttle bus, which runs regularly during these months. For shuttle schedules, contact the Aspen Ranger District at (970) 925-3445 or visit the Aspen office at 806 West Hallam. Restrooms, picnic facilities, and information are available at the trailhead.

Key points:
0.0 Trailhead.
0.5 Pass the wilderness sign on the Maroon-Snowmass Trail.
1.3 Meet the Maroon Lake Scenic Trail.
1.5 Cross the bridge over Maroon Creek.

The hike: Classic Colorado. Simple and clear, Maroon Lake is classic Colorado. This is the picture on the postcards—the Maroon Bells clad in ribbons of snow during winter, skirted in greenery and wildflowers in summer, and set off by the electric yellows of the changing aspen in autumn, all reflected postcard picture perfect in the still waters of Maroon Lake. You can place yourself front and center by hiking the Maroon Lake Scenic Trail.

None of the braided trails around Maroon Lake are backbreakers, but the farther you travel toward the Bells, the more work you will do. A ten-minute ramble through soft meadow to the blue shore of the tarn, or a climb through whispering aspen that tests the lungs and knees—it's your choice.

The route described here climbs above the lake. A brief plunge through the forest lands you adjacent to the lake's inlet stream, and a meander through the dense undergrowth bordering the stream and beaver ponds drops you into the meadowland near the trailhead. You do not, however, have to follow the described loop; you can stay low on the more popular figure-eight loop. Given the steepness of the down-hill section, however, you would be wise to complete the described loop in a counterclockwise direction.

Leaving the bus stop, the trail leads up to the right (southwest), through the meadow above Maroon Lake. Aspen cluster around the path. At the trail intersection, go right (southwest) on the Maroon-Snowmass Trail (#1975) and begin to climb. The trail flattens as it passes the upper reaches of Maroon Lake. At the wilderness sign near the 0.5-mile mark, stay right (southwest) on the Maroon-Snowmass Trail.

The trail crosses a rockslide and continues to climb. At the next trail crossing, at about the 1-mile mark, go left (south), leaving the Maroon-Snowmass Trail and descending into the trees. The trail gets steep and rocky as it drops down the switchbacks. At about 1.3 miles, you will reach another trail intersection; go left (northeast) on the Maroon Lake Scenic Trail to the beaver ponds.

The trail wanders down through dense, waist-high undergrowth thick with wildflowers and bugs in June and early July, when snowmelt moistens the earth and feeds the cataracts and waterfalls along the creek. Cross the bridge over West Maroon Creek at 1.5 miles, and follow the south side of the creek to a second bridge near the head of the lake. Go straight across the bridge, sticking to the waterside path.

Social trails wander through the meadows around Maroon Lake. Try to stick to the designated trail—or the trail best traveled—to minimize erosion and damage to this fragile and overused ecosystem. The trail leads up and left (northeast) to broad stairs that climb to the parking area at about 2 miles.

12
CRATER LAKE

see map page 52

Type of hike: Out-and-back.
Total distance: 3.6 miles.
Elevation change: 496 feet.
Maps: USGS Maroon Bells; National Geographic/Trails Illustrated Maroon Bells, Redstone, Marble; Aspen, Crested Butte and Gunnison Recreation Topo Map by Latitude 40.
Jurisdiction: Maroon Bells–Snowmass Wilderness, White River National Forest.

Finding the trailhead: Parking at Maroon Lake can be accessed during the summer only before 8:30 A.M., when Maroon Creek Road is open to traffic, or anytime during the snow-free months of spring and autumn. From the roundabout, follow Maroon Creek Road (Colorado Highway 13) southwest for about 10.5 miles to its end at West Maroon Portal. If you start after 8:30 A.M. between mid-June and September, you will have to take the shuttle bus, which runs regularly during these months. For shuttle schedules, contact the Aspen Ranger District at (970) 925-3445 or visit the Aspen office at 806 West Hallam. Restrooms, picnic facilities, and information are available at the trailhead.

Key points:
0.0 Trailhead.
0.5 Pass the wilderness sign and continue up on the Maroon-Snowmass Trail.
1.0 Pass the intersection with the trail leading down to Maroon Lake.
1.5 Gain a view of Crater Lake.
1.8 Reach the shores of Crater Lake.

The hike: Even in the warm, reassuring light of the summer sun, the Maroon Bells are imposing. The crumbling red rock rises in well-defined layers to the pointed summits—there is clearly no easy way to the top. So why bother? This hike will take you to a shallow lake fed by snowmelt from the awesome Bells, whose magnificence is just as inspiring from the lake's peaceful shores. Should you be concerned that you are not meeting the challenge of the surrounding peaks, fear not: The hike is steep in spots, and you will have earned the spectacular views.

The trail begins by circling the western shore of Maroon Lake, then climbs the headwall at the southern end of the valley to the basin that cradles Crater Lake. Headwall is an intimidating word, but it's a brief climb, and more than worth the effort.

Depart from the parking lot on the highest path that wanders through the wildflowers on the western shore of Maroon Lake. Wander through aspen groves to the Maroon-Snowmass Trail (#1975); take this trail to the right (southwest) and begin to climb.

The trail levels as it reaches the head of Maroon Lake. At the Maroon Bells–Snowmass Wilderness sign at about 0.5 mile, continue right (southwest) on the Maroon-Snowmass Trail. The route traverses a rockslide, then meets the path that leads steeply downhill to the Maroon Lake Scenic Trail at 1 mile. Continue up and right (southwest) on the Maroon-Snowmass Trail.

The path crosses beneath the rocky moraine that guards the head of the valley, then wanders back through aspen, climbing two switchbacks. At the top of the rock debris, the trail becomes a rocky but easy roller coaster. The Bells and a small waterfall command your attention.

At about 1.5 miles, the trail crests a hill and begins to descend. Crater Lake pops into view, then is shielded by a grove of aspen. At the trail intersection above the lake, take West Maroon Trail (#1970) to the left (south), toward the lakeshore. A short walk through low scrub and wildflowers lands you waterside at 1.8 miles.

Return as you came.

Option: Once you reach the web of trails around Maroon Lake on your return from Crater Lake, you can vary your route back to the parking area. See the Maroon Lake Scenic Trail (Hike 11) for a description of some of these trails.

13
CATHEDRAL LAKE

Type of hike: Out-and-back.
Total distance: 6.4 miles.
Elevation change: 1,986 feet.
Maps: USGS Hayden Peak; National Geographic/Trails Illustrated Aspen, Independence Pass; Aspen, Crested Butte and Gunnison Recreation Topo Map by Latitude 40.
Trail number: 1984.
Jurisdiction: Maroon Bells–Snowmass Wilderness, White River National Forest.
Special considerations: You risk being hit by lightning at Cathedral Lake; descend immediately if a thunderstorm threatens. The elevation of the lake also necessitates an awareness of the potential for altitude sickness to develop.

Finding the trailhead: From the roundabout, head south on Castle Creek Road for 12 miles to the signed road to the Cathedral Lake Trailhead. Turn right (west) on the gravel access road and drive 0.5 mile to the parking area and the trailhead proper.

Key points:
0.0 Trailhead.
0.7 Encounter a series of overlooks near the wilderness boundary.
1.5 Reach the waterfall overlook.

Cathedral Lake

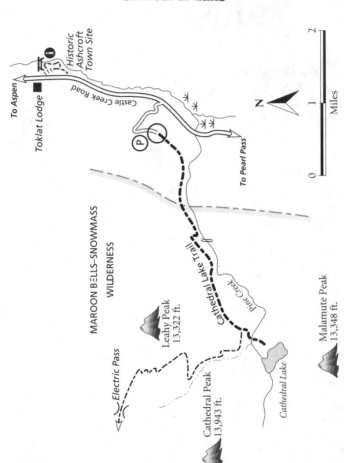

To Aspen

Toklat Lodge

Historic Ashcroft Town Site

Castle Creek Road

To Pearl Pass

P

N

Miles

0   1   2

MAROON BELLS-SNOWMASS WILDERNESS

Electric Pass

Leahy Peak
13,322 ft.

Cathedral Lake Trail

Pine Creek

Cathedral Peak
13,943 ft.

Cathedral Lake

Malamute Peak
13,348 ft.

2.5 Cross the second talus field and ascend steep switch-backs.

3.2 Arrive on the shores of Cathedral Lake.

The hike: The craggy, eroded spires of Cathedral Peak and the sweep of alpine tundra leading up to Electric Pass corral Cathedral Lake. Huddled beneath the arcing mountain, sheltered by its heights, the lake's sparsely veg-etated basin is open to the east, where the distant Collegiate Range forms an imposing horizon. The trail leading up to the tarn is as rugged as its goal, but the reward is respite on the rocky shore of a lake visited most often by marmots, pikas, and soaring hawks.

The route begins with a moderately steep, traversing climb up the aspen-covered east-facing wall of the Castle Creek canyon. Curving into the Pine Creek drainage, which it follows most of the way to Cathedral Lake, the trail offers views up the Castle Creek valley that slowly disappear as you ascend.

At about 0.7 mile, the trail's pitch mellows and the aspen thin out. A small footpath breaks off to the left (south) to an overlook rock with more views of the Castle Creek canyon. About 100 feet farther, another overlook in a stand of evergreens allows you to peer down at the rush-ing Pine Creek. Pass the wilderness sign, and enjoy a number of views of the Pine Creek gorge as you ascend.

The aspens thin out and become no higher than shrubs as you enter a basin full of wildflowers throughout the hik-ing season. Steep cliffs flank the trail, and at about 1.5

miles, as you continue upward, a waterfall comes into view. Round a couple of switchbacks, then Pine Creek, tumbling through its dark-rock gorge, is your companion on a long traverse.

Climb two more switchbacks, and the pitch of the climb again mellows as gigantic twin cirques open before you. Cross a talus field to the top of the headwall, where absolutely stunning views both northwest and southeast await. The creek rumbles below, with a cave or mine adit tucked in the southeast wall of the draw.

The ascent eases into a meadowy meander as you skirt the south-facing wall of a high valley, its rocks glassy in the sunshine. Climb into another pika-chirpy talus field at about 2.5 miles, then excruciatingly steep switchbacks, first in the open, then wedged between trees and a crumbling rock outcrop, lead up the next headwall. Pass a sign admonishing against cutting the switchbacks (as if you could). When you rest, you can check out the expansive views to the southeast.

At the top of the headwall, you will meet the trail to Electric Pass, which breaks off to the right (north). The trail to Cathedral Lake leads to the left (southwest), descending across a bridge in an alpine marsh. Pass a nice campsite (where a sign prohibits fires) on the left (south); stay right, and climb over a shrubby hump to the next trail sign alongside the creek. Again, Cathedral Lake is to the left (south), and Electric Pass is to the right (north).

A split-log bridge spans the creek, then the trail climbs up and over rolling hummocks, leaving the trees behind.

Cathedral Peak, at 13,943 feet, looms ahead; a faint trail switchbacks up the clean slope on your right (north) to Electric Pass. At 3.2 miles you drop to the lake, cupped beneath ragged ramparts of gray-pink rock stained with black streaks. The lake is stormy blue, skirted entirely by talus and the low-growing willow, tufted grasses, and stunted flowers typical of alpine tundra.

Enjoy your stay at the lake, then return as you came.

Options: If you want to climb higher, you can venture upward on the Electric Pass Trail, which leads to the steep divide between Cathedral Peak and Hayden Peak.

14
HISTORIC ASHCROFT BOARDWALK

Type of hike: Loop.
Total distance: 0.6 mile.
Elevation change: Minimal.
Maps: USGS Hayden Peak; National Geographic/Trails Illustrated Aspen, Independence Pass; Aspen, Crested Butte and Gunnison Recreation Topo Map by Latitude 40.
Jurisdiction: White River National Forest.
Special considerations: A small fee is levied to tour the site.

Finding the trailhead: From the roundabout, head south on Castle Creek Road. The Ashcroft Townsite is located 11 miles up the Castle Creek Road. Plenty of parking is available, along with a privy, picnic facilities, and information.

Key points:
0.0 Trailhead.
0.2 Head down to the creek.
0.4 Reach the picnic area.
0.6 Climb back to the boardwalk.

The hike: A visit to the boardwalk and trail at the Ashcroft Townsite more than qualifies as one of the best easy sojourns in the Aspen area. Set in a spectacular alpine valley, the trail wanders through colorful meadows and along-

Historic Ashcroft Boardwalk

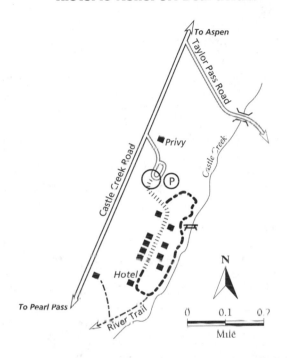

side playful Castle Creek, leading from historic building to interpretive sign and back to historic building. So easy some might argue it is more a stroll than a hike, its setting and history conspire to make the Ashcroft loop worthwhile.

Ashcroft's story mirrors that of many Colorado mining boomtowns gone bust. Before silver was discovered in the surrounding mountains, the site, cozied up along the meadowy banks of Castle Creek, was a summer hunting ground for a band of Ute Indians. In 1880, prospectors from the Leadville area discovered silver deposits in the valley, and established Castle Forks City, which was later renamed Ashcroft.

The mining camp, fed by a steady stream of fortune seekers, grew quickly, reaching a peak population of 2,500 by the middle of the 1880s. Among its transient residents were famed Colorado mining mogul Horace Tabor, who, with his wife Baby Doe, built a cabin in the area and participated in the establishment of Ashcroft's smelter.

The boom faded as the veins were depleted: By 1890, both men and businesses abandoned the lovely site and followed the siren song of quick riches to shining new towns, including nearby Aspen. A handful of miners remained however, breathing faint life into the fading town. And though the area never again saw (nor likely will see) the activity of its heyday, its setting prompted Olympian Billy Fiske and his partners to plan a ski resort development in the area. Ashcroft also served as a training ground for the famed skiing warriors of the 10th Mountain Division, and was the backdrop for movies and television shows. In 1974, the Aspen Historical Society, in cooperation with the Forest Service, succeeded in establishing Ashcroft as a National Register Historic Site, and the society has maintained the site's ghost town integrity ever since.

The townsite's history is elaborated on in both a fact sheet available through the Forest Service and in an Aspen Historical Society brochure available at the information booth/tent at the trailhead. You will also be asked to pay a small fee at the trailhead; the money is used to maintain the trail and buildings.

The trail is well maintained and easy to follow. Head south out of the parking lot, picking up the boardwalk that leads through the heart of the town and keeps visitors out of the meadowland, which are rich with wildflowers through the summer months. Interpretive signs line the boardwalk, describing the work of ecologist, preservationist, and dog sled aficionado Stuart Mace; the Ute tribe that hunted in the area; and other subjects.

Round a bend to the southwest and enter the ghost town proper. Footpaths lead from the boardwalk to the buildings, which include the Blue Mirror Saloon (there were 16 to 20 saloons in the town at its height), the post office (which operated for a scant 10 years), and a number of cabins and business establishments. Interpretive signs identify the buildings, describe how the town was laid out, and include poignant details of life in this dynamic and isolated setting.

At about 0.2 mile, at the hotel, turn left (east) and head down the path to the creek. Interpretive signs on this stretch of trail range from a description of the prehistoric Timberline Man to the sled dogs of Toklat. The path intersects the River Trail, which leads right to the Pine Creek Cookhouse; turn left (north) and follow the overgrown path alongside the rambling creek, passing more interpretive signs as you proceed. At about 0.4 mile, you reach a picnic area with a fire pit, and other great picnic sites along the creek. Stay right (north), passing the picnic sites and following the creek to the next interpretive sign, which describes ranching and farming in the valley. The trail curves sharply left (west) and climbs gently back toward the boardwalk, passing a decrepit wagon and a last interpretive sign describing defunct plans to establish a ski resort at the site. Once back on the boardwalk, turn right; the parking lot and trailhead is at about 0.6 mile.

Option: If this just doesn't satisfy your urge to hike, you can combine this path with a challenging climb to Cathedral Lake (Hike 13).

15
DIFFICULT CREEK TRAIL

Type of hike: Out-and-back.
Total distance: 4 miles.
Elevation change: 1,090 feet.
Maps: USGS Aspen and Hayden Peak; National Geographic/Trails Illustrated Aspen, Independence Pass; Aspen, Crested Butte and Gunnison Recreation Topo Map by Latitude 40.
Trail number: 2196.
Jurisdiction: Collegiate Peaks Wilderness, White River National Forest.

Finding the trailhead: From the roundabout, head east on Colorado Highway 82, through the town of Aspen (where the highway doubles as Main Street). Continue out of town on CO 82, traveling 4 miles from the intersection of Main and Mill Streets to the Difficult Campground sign. Go right (southeast) at the sign, and drive 0.6 mile on the Difficult Campground access road to the sign for the picnic and day-use area. Go right into the picnic area parking lot; the trailhead is at the east end of the lot.

Key points:
0.0 Trailhead.
1.5 Reach the third stand of aspen.
2.0 Arrive in the streamside dell.

Difficult Creek Trail

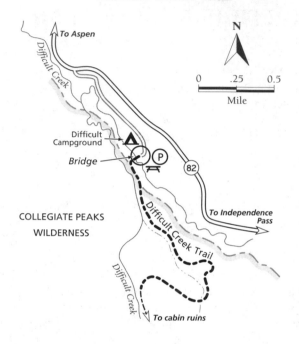

The hike: Imagine yourself wrapped in a warm green blanket of aspen and evergreens, serenaded by a laughing wind, nourished by ripe red berries and the clear water of a mountain spring. The Difficult Creek Trail is swaddled in such a natural environment (varying with the season); pick a sunny late-summer afternoon and revel in the colors, the swirling sounds, and the peace.

You will have to work for your sun-splashed idyll, however—the Difficult Creek Trail is a good, solid climb. The trail's ultimate destination is the remains of four old cabins, tucked in the woods along the creek, but this hike ends in a shady dell flushed by silvery Difficult Creek, where the trees grow openly enough to allow the sunshine through. The trail climbs through a forest of great variety; in late summer, wild berries grow thick along its edges.

At its outset, the trail is flat and meanders through the riparian habitat at creekside. Go left (southeast) at the trail fork (following the signs), and cross a dirt road. Beyond, you cross the bridge that spans the Roaring Fork River. The trail bears right (downstream), then switchbacks onto a sage-covered mini-mesa. Stay on the best used path, bearing southeast (up the valley).

The trail climbs through aspens to a lovely flat spot beside tumbling Difficult Creek, flattening in a patch of wild raspberries. Then a steep, rocky climb alongside the stream begins; the trail levels briefly in a forest of fir and spruce, then climbs through an aspen stand.

As you pass the half-mile mark, the trail's pitch eases and its surface becomes sandy. Again, you will enter a grand grove of aspen, some of which arc over the trail. By the third stand of aspen, at about 1.5 miles, the sounds of the creek and its tributaries have been left behind.

Cross a gully thick with berries, then pass the foot of a rockslide. The trail ascends a switchback, and levels in evergreens before climbing again. Round a wide corner into a stand of lodgepoles. The trail levels as it skirts a ravine that harbors huge, old-growth aspen, and proceeds to the creek, which is cradled in a parkland of aspen and pine at 2 miles. Rest in this lush, cool dell; you can turn around here, or continue up if the mood is right.

When you chose to return to the trailhead, walk lightly—it is all downhill from here.

Option: The Difficult Creek Trail continues beyond the dell, climbing alongside its namesake, to the cabin ruins. Beyond the cabins, the trail is not maintained.

16
WELLER LAKE TRAIL

Type of hike: Out-and-back.
Total distance: 1.2 miles.
Elevation change: 300 feet.
Maps: USGS New York Peak; National Geographic/Trails Illustrated Aspen, Independence Pass; Aspen, Crested Butte and Gunnison Recreation Topo Map by Latitude 40.
Trail number: 1989.
Jurisdiction: Collegiate Peaks Wilderness, White River National Forest.

Finding the trailhead: From the roundabout, head east on Colorado Highway 82 through the town of Aspen (where the highway doubles as Main Street). Continue out of town on CO 82, traveling 8.4 miles from the intersection of Main and Mill Streets to the signs for Weller Campground. The trailhead parking area is on the right (south) side of the road, opposite the campground.

Key points:
0.0 Trailhead.
0.5 Cross a footbridge.
0.6 Reach Weller Lake.

The hike: Like yin and yang, the two faces of Weller Lake are opposites, yet harmonize perfectly. On the south-

73

Weller Lake Trail
The Grottos

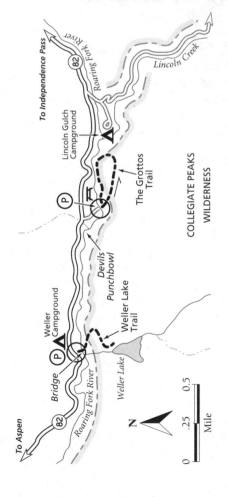

and west-facing slopes a thick forest grows; on the north- and east-facing slopes, the naked rock skeleton of the mountains disdains flora, and a broad swatch of dead trees stretches up toward the gray summits. A soft seat on the duff that forms the floor of the campsite at the north end of the lake is the perfect place to contemplate this juxtaposition.

The Weller Lake Trail climbs steadily through forest to its destination, but it's not particularly steep. If by serendipity you walk this path in autumn, you will catch fiery aspen trees at their best, painting the sunlight amber and dropping circlets of gold on the brown path.

Stairs lead down and out of the east end of the aspen-shrouded parking area. At the trail sign, bear right (west); the path drops quickly to the Roaring Fork River. The trail intersects a social path; stay right, moving away from the river, then curving back to the water.

Follow the meandering route through high grasses to a bridge that spans the Roaring Fork; cross the bridge and climb the stairs on its south side to a Weller Lake Trail sign. Go right (southwest) on the Weller Lake Trail (the path to the left leads a short distance to a platform overlooking the Roaring Fork); the trail crosses a footbridge over a gully.

Pass a sign marking the boundaries of the Collegiate Peaks Wilderness and the White River National Forest. Climb three gentle switchbacks; at the fourth switchback, the forest is a little thinner, and the trail gets a little rockier. Cross another footbridge at about the 0.5-mile mark.

The path rounds another switchback and climbs through yet another grove of aspen. Ascend the final, easy pitch to the north shore of the lake, which sits in a bowl at the base of New York and Difficult Peaks. The naked trunks of dead trees clutter the south shore; a narrow fisherman's trail leads around the east shore to a narrow beach at 0.6 mile.

Once you've enjoyed the lake (and, possibly, caught a few fish), descend to the parking area as you came.

17
THE GROTTOS

see map page 74

Type of hike: Various loop options.
Total distance: 1 mile, more or less.
Elevation change: Minimal.
Maps: USGS New York Peak; National Geographic/Trails Illustrated Aspen, Independence Pass; Aspen, Crested Butte and Gunnison Recreation Topo Map by Latitude 40.
Trail number: 2180.
Jurisdiction: Collegiate Peaks Wilderness, White River National Forest.

Finding the trailhead: From the roundabout, head east on Colorado Highway 82 through Aspen. Continue east of Aspen on CO 82, traveling 9.3 miles from the intersection of Mill and Main Streets to a dirt road that drops right (south) off of the highway. The access road is marked with a sign that reads "Grottos Day Use Area." (The road is approximately 0.9 mile past the Weller Campground. CO 82 narrows beyond the Grottos entry; if you reach this, you have gone too far.) Turn right (south) on the dirt road, and follow it to its end at the parking area.

Key points:
0.0 Trailhead.
0.5 Reach the end of the Old Stage Road.
1.0 Reach the fishing dock at the river trail.

The hike: From the ice cave to the "erratic boulders" scattered helter-skelter on a smooth granite table, from the grand mixed forests that line the Old Stage Road to the warm flat rocks that overlook the narrows of the Roaring Fork, The Grottos are enchanting.

Describing a route through this popular area is tough, but the map near the trailhead shows some of the possibilities. The Old Stage Road, which forms the bulk of this description, is wide and obvious. Once the road reaches the rim of the Roaring Fork canyon, however, trails branch in all directions. These braided trails wreak havoc on the environment, so try to stick to the path best traveled. Stay close to the Roaring Fork; from the riverside path, you will see the falls. And feel free to diverge from the route described below; none of the trails are so long or obscure that you can get lost.

To begin, cross the bridge over the Roaring Fork (a good fishing spot) and pass the informational sign describing The Grottos. Head up the willow-lined Old Stage Road, passing "erratic boulders" balanced precariously on an ice-scoured granite slab. At the trail fork, stay right and climb gently on the Old Stage Road.

Emerge from the woods at a large granite slab, where you will find the wagon road built up on granite talus. Circle into the woods again at about 0.2 mile.

At about 0.3 mile, the trail parallels a narrow canyon of rock with steep but shallow walls. By 0.5 mile, the Old Stage Road has ended near Lincoln Creek, which shortly enters the Roaring Fork River.

From here, follow the path that curves left (north) into the trees, then hooks farther left (west). Ramble through the open woods to a wonderful little bay on the Roaring Fork River. Follow one of the braided paths up over slabs, staying close to the river, and continue to a rocky waterfall overlook at about 0.8 mile. The road to Independence Pass hugs the lip of a ledge carved into the steep wall on the north side of the river.

A prominent path (wander around, you will find it) leads down and left (southwest), over several fallen trees and past a small fire pit, then merges with a well-trod route that stays close to the river. The shoreline path leads to a beach, fishing dock, and picnic area off the river trail at about 1 mile. Follow the trail left (south) away from the beach; at the trail fork, go right (west) onto the Old Stage Road. Head right (down and west) to return to the parking area.

Options: As mentioned above, there are many trails to explore in The Grottos. The ice cave can be reached by veering left off the Old Stage Road on an unmarked path, and other paths lead to wonderful picnic sites and climbing boulders scattered in the woods. Explore and enjoy.

18

DISCOVERY AND BRAILLE TRAILS

Type of hike: Two short loops.
Total distance: 0.25 mile for each loop.
Elevation change: Minimal.
Maps: USGS Thimble Rock and New York Peak; National Geographic/Trails Illustrated Aspen and Independence Pass; Aspen, Crested Butte and Gunnison Recreation Topo Map by Latitude 40. The trail does not appear on all maps.
Jurisdiction: White River National Forest.

Finding the trailhead: From the roundabout, take Colorado Highway 82 east, through the town of Aspen, and climb the road toward Independence Pass for about 13 miles. The marked trailhead is on the right (south) side of the road. Picnic sites are available near the parking area.

Key points:
0.0 Trailhead.
0.2 Approach the end of the Discovery Trail.
0.5 Complete the Braille Trail.

The hike: Look closely. See the subtle differences in color and structure that separate the spruce from the fir from the pine. Watch for trout in the sun-splashed Roaring Fork River.

Discovery and Braille Trails

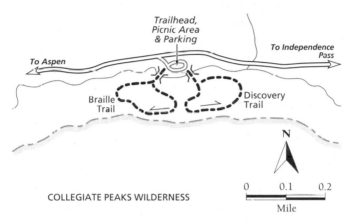

Trailhead,
Picnic Area
& Parking

To Independence
Pass

To Aspen

Braille
Trail

Discovery
Trail

N

COLLEGIATE PEAKS WILDERNESS

0   0.1   0.2

Mile

Observe the the trail surface as it changes from rock to duff to hard dirt. Everything you see is vivid and crisp at this altitude, outlined as sharply as comic book characters.

Now close your eyes. Clasp the thin rope that guides you through the same forest, and experience instead the different smells and textures of spruce, fir, and pine, the sound of the wind as it stirs the boughs high above, the uncertain and ever-changing feel of the trail beneath your feet.

If you have your sight, these twin interpretive trails enable you to experience the mountains in entirely different ways. If you are blind, the Braille Trail offers unique experiential interpretation of the subalpine wilderness below Independence Pass. Signs along both short routes describe the forest and riparian habitats that trim the adolescent Roaring Fork River as it spills toward Aspen.

Begin on the Discovery Trail, which is on the left (east) side of the parking area and is wheelchair accessible. Head right (southeast) on the gravel path into the woodlands to picnic benches and tables. The Roaring Fork sparkles before you; a bench and interpretive sign to your right overlook the river. Continue to the left into the woods, heading around the loop in a counterclockwise direction. Pass another bench, a blank interpretive sign, and more picnic tables. The lodgepoles grow thickly here.

A switchback is wedged between two interpretive signs (the second blank as of this writing); the next interpretive sign discusses the trees of the ecosystem. Pass a final bench, switchback, and interpretive sign, and follow a straight section of trail to the parking lot at 0.25 mile.

The Braille Trail begins on the right (west) side of the parking lot. A wire traces the path, and interpretive signs in both Braille and English are provided.

Pass three interpretive signs before you cross a wide bridge over the Roaring Fork. Beyond the bridge the trail forks; go left (clockwise) to follow the signs, which encourage hikers to feel the softness of the forest floor, differences in the textures of bark, the scales of lichens, the coolness of mosses, and the smells of water and bog. There are 22 signs in all, each revealing an unseen aspect of the woodlands.

The trail is relatively flat and easy, but does sport typical mountain hiking obstacles for both sighted and blind hikers: rocks, roots, twists, and turns. Travel slowly and with care.

Return to the bridge, and then the parking area, at about 0.5 mile.

19

INDEPENDENCE TOWNSITE

Type of hike: Loop.
Total distance: 1 mile, more or less.
Elevation change: Minimal.
Maps: USGS Independence Pass; National Geographic/Trails Illustrated Aspen, Independence Pass; Aspen, Crested Butte and Gunnison Recreation Topo Map by Latitude 40.
Jurisdiction: White River National Forest.

Finding the trailhead: From the roundabout, head east on Colorado Highway 82 through Aspen (the highway doubles as Main Street in town). Continue east of Aspen on CO 82, traveling 16 miles from the intersection of Mill and Main Streets to the Independence Townsite, which is on the right (south) side of the highway.

Key points:
0.0 Trailhead.
0.5 Reach the west edge of town.
1.0 Climb back to the trailhead.

The hike: The remnants of the mining town of Independence huddle high on the Roaring Fork River. At nearly 11,000 feet, the summer sun barely warms the stiff winds blowing down from the Continental Divide. These

83

Independence Townsite

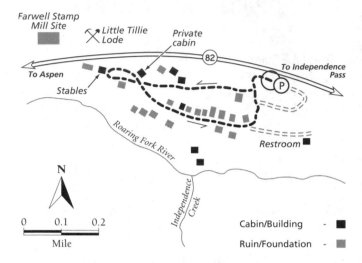

winds whip through the timbers of the buildings that remain standing and blast over the rotting foundations of those that have collapsed, stirring up images of how the harshness of the landscape must have been reflected in the lives of the men who worked here.

Among the first mining towns established in the mountains outside Aspen, legend has it Independence was founded on July 4, 1879. As with many other boomtowns, Independence blossomed quickly; by 1882, the town boasted more than 40 businesses and a thousand residents. The bloom faded quickly too; by the late 1880s Independence was well on its way to becoming a lonely ghost town.

The very short loop described here is but one of several you can follow through the townsite. Though the trail is very short, plan to spend a morning or afternoon exploring the ruins, lingering in the doorways of long-unused buildings, learning about the lives and times of those who once lived in this harsh environment.

Begin by walking down the stairs on the west side of the parking lot and past an interpretive sign. At the first trail intersection, head right (west), passing above the first ruin. Walk above foundations cradled in the wind-blown grasses to a well-preserved structure held together with square nails. The trail skirts a private residence and its outhouse, then heads past the "ghost's" residence.

Drop onto the road in front of a collapsed cabin of bleached timbers. A short trail to the left leads to a leaning two-room cabin with a front porch and a deep pit in the south wing.

Return to the main path/road and head downhill to two more structures. The second, at about the 0.5-mile mark, looks as though it was blown apart—its stud walls lie on the road. Pass the relatively well-preserved stable; a trail leads down from here toward the Roaring Fork River, where still more ruins retain a tenuous hold against the elements. Views south open into an avalanche chute on Independence Mountain.

Continue east up the road to a picnic bench; the trail parallels the frigid headwaters of the Roaring Fork. Pass another outhouse; the trail curves back north toward the parking lot. Cross a shallow ditch and climb to the pavement at about 1 mile.

20
LINKINS LAKE TRAIL

Type of hike: Out-and-back.
Total distance: 1.2 miles.
Elevation change: 502 feet.
Maps: USGS Independence Pass and Mount Champion; National Geographic/Trails Illustrated Aspen, Independence Pass; Aspen, Crested Butte and Gunnison Recreation Topo Map by Latitude 40.
Trail number: 1979.
Jurisdiction: Hunter-Fryingpan Wilderness, White River National Forest.
Special considerations: If you are caught in a thunderstorm at Linkins Lake, you risk being struck by lightning. If dark clouds threaten, retreat to the safety of your vehicle immediately. Altitude is another factor on this hike—the lake lies at more than 12,000 feet. Watch members of your hiking party carefully for signs of altitude sickness, and descend immediately if symptoms manifest themselves.

Finding the trailhead: From the roundabout, head east on Colorado Highway 82 through Aspen (the highway doubles as Main Street in town). Continue east of Aspen on CO 82 to the last switchback before the Independence Pass summit at about 18.1 miles. The trail begins from a turnout on the left (north) side of the road.

Linkins Lake Trail

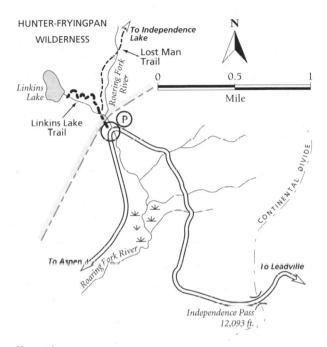

Key points:
0.0 Trailhead.
0.1 Pass the Lost Man Trail junction.
0.6 Arrive at Linkins Lake.

The hike: Perched near the lip of a hanging valley overlooking the headwaters of the Roaring Fork River, Linkins

Lake is an alpine tarn of the first order. Gem green and piercingly clear, it is clothed in the fragile flowers, grasses, and lichen that cling to the wind-whipped earth above treeline, and is guarded by the mighty Continental Divide. Tread lightly, and revel in the altitude. You will never see a lake more icily perfect, or mountains etched so dramatically against a deep-blue sky.

The trail into the hanging valley that holds the lake is short but steep, and the air is very thin. Take your time and enjoy the views while you catch your breath.

Leave the roadside parking area and begin hiking uphill to the north through low-growing shrubs. At the intersection with the Lost Man Trail (#1996), which branches to the right (north) at 0.1 mile, go left (northwest) on the Linkins Lake Trail. Head up through the willows, then hop rocks across the lake's small outlet stream.

The trail ascends through clusters of wind-stunted subalpine fir that may be 200 years old. The trail flattens briefly, offering views up the barren and beautiful valley that holds Lost Man Trail and Independence Lake.

Cross a streamlet, then climb to a rocky switchback that swings the trail and the views south and west. The trail forks into social paths at a rock outcrop; head left (south) to surmount this steep, rocky section. The trail flattens on the edge of the Linkins Lake basin. A short, easy descent through alpine tundra drops you to the margin of the lake, green and precious as jade, at 0.6 mile.

La Plata Peak dominates views to the south as you descend the same path you climbed. Keep your eyes on the trail; the footing is trickier going down than it is going up.